LEONARDO DA VINCI

The quintessential Renaissance man

Written by Tatiana Sgalbiero
In collaboration with Julie Piront
Translated by Emma Hanna

Art & Literature   50MINUTES.com

LEONARDO DA VINCI   9

CONTEXT   13

The Italian Renaissance
The Republic of Florence
Rivalry with Milan and Rome
The Italian Wars

BIOGRAPHY   23

Apprenticeship in Florence
Travelling to Milan
Return to Florence
Retirement in France

CHARACTERISTICS OF DA VINCI'S WORK   33

Verrocchio's influence
Painting as a science
Major technical innovations

NOTABLE WORKS   41

The Last Supper
The *Mona Lisa*
Virgin of the Rocks
The Virgin and Child with St. Anne

DA VINCI'S LEGACY   59

SUMMARY   65

FURTHER READING   71

LEONARDO DA VINCI

- **Name:** Leonardo di ser Piero da Vinci.
- **Born:** 15 April 1452 in Vinci, Tuscany (Italy).
- **Died:** 2 May 1519 in Clos Lucé, near Amboise (France).
- **Context:** the Italian Renaissance.
- **Notable works:**
  - *Annunciation* (1472-1475)
  - *Adoration of the Magi* (1481-1482)
  - *Virgin of the Rocks* (1483-1486)
  - *The Last Supper* (1494-1498)
  - *Mona Lisa* (1503-1505)
  - *The Virgin and Child with St. Anne* (c. 1510)

Although many famous polymaths were active during the Italian Renaissance, Leonardo da Vinci stands above the rest due to the sheer quantity of disciplines he worked in and mastered over the course of his life, including painting, sculpture, architecture, hydraulics, optics, mathematics, botany, military engineering, anatomy and physics. He was a true genius, and produced stunning artwork, incredible sketches and all kinds of inventions, some of which were so ahead of his time that they were never actually built until the modern era. He kept track of his work in notebooks which numbered over 7000 pages in total, although many of them have been lost over the years and the remainder have been scattered across the world.

Da Vinci travelled a great deal over the course of his life, particularly in northern and central Italy and in France, which allowed him to meet many of the most influential figures of the era: the Italian artists Donato Bramante (1444-1514), Sandro Botticelli (1445-1510), Domenico Ghirlandaio (1449-1494), Michelangelo (1475-1564) and Raphael (1483-1520); the writer Niccolò Machiavelli (1469-1527); Pope Leo X (1475-1521); the ruler of Florence, Lorenzo de' Medici (1449-1492); the Duke of Milan, Ludovico Sforza (1452-1508); the Italian nobleman Cesare Borgia (1475-1507); and the French King Francis I (1494-1547).

His work had such a tremendous influence on the society he lived in that there is a clear distinction between the periods "before" and "after" da Vinci in the fields of art and engineering. This is particularly true of the field of painting, as da Vinci is credited with developing a number of new techniques, such as *sfumato* and atmospheric perspective. But even though da Vinci was the driving force behind artistic innovation in the late 15th and early 16th centuries, he also encountered a number of difficulties: he never enjoyed an easy relationship with any of his artistic patrons, who even included the French King Francis I, as he was generally unable to strike a balance between complying with their demands and fulfilling his own artistic vision. This is undoubtedly the reason why so many of his works are unfinished and remain shrouded in a degree of mystery.

CONTEXT

THE ITALIAN RENAISSANCE

The Renaissance began in the Italian city of Florence in the mid-15th century, and spread across the rest of Europe over the course of the 16th century. This tremendously influential movement was born from the study of ancient Greek and Latin texts, which led to the rediscovery of many artistic and cultural principles dating from antiquity. Its aims were to revive these traditions and restore learning and knowledge to a more prominent position within society. The great thinkers of the era also began placing greater emphasis on the inherent value of humanity, particularly through the idea that human beings could improve themselves by gaining knowledge. As such, it was a time of research and discovery, which led to innovation in a wide range of scientific and artistic fields. For example, the new theories on perspective and proportions that were developed by sculptors and architects had a tremendous influence on artistic techniques.

Artists also began to receive a great deal more recognition for their work: they began signing their artwork with their names and were no longer considered mere artisans. Furthermore, they began drawing inspiration from different sources, notably from ancient Greek and Roman mythology, and secular works such as portraits, nudes and mythological allegories became much more popular. Italian nobles also realised that art could be used as a tool to glorify themselves or their cities, and patronage became a much more common practice. This meant that artists received more commissions, which in turn bolstered their reputations.

DID YOU KNOW?

Unlike other great thinkers of his time, da Vinci did not base his work on classical principles, and even admitted that he was unfamiliar with them in his writings. On the contrary, his painting style was primarily influenced by his own worldview, which was based on his life experience and scientific experiments. In a way, it could be said that he did not believe anything unless he had seen it with his own eyes.

THE REPUBLIC OF FLORENCE

Italy did not become a unified country until 1870, and was made up of a variety of city-states in the 15th century. One of these cities was Florence, which was ruled by the wealthy Medici family from 1434 onwards. Under their leadership, the city entered a golden age of political, economic and cultural prosperity, and notably became the central hub of artistic production on the Italian peninsula under the guidance of Lorenzo de' Medici, also known as Lorenzo the Magnificent. The greatest artists and philosophers of the era flocked to the city, but Lorenzo's death in 1492 plunged the metropolis into a period of crisis which lasted until 1494, when his son Piero II (1472-1503) was banished from the city. This marked the beginning of a period of exile for the Medici family which lasted until 1512.

Furthermore, the King of France, Charles VIII (1470-1498), set out to conquer the Duchy of Milan and the Kingdom of Naples in 1494, and also conquered Florence that year. Fear spread through the city, reinforced by the surging belief in millenarianism, a doctrine that claimed the world would end at the turn of the century (in other words, in 1500). The preacher Girolamo Savonarola (1452-1498) took advantage of this climate of fear to call for a return to austerity, and set up "bonfires of the vanities" where books, paintings, jewellery and any other objects that he deemed to be a source of vanity could be publicly burned. However, these practices drew the ire of the Florentine authorities and of Pope Alexander VI (1431-1503), and he was executed in Florence in 1498.

In 1502, the city's prior Piero Soderini (1450-1522) was elected *gonfaloniere* for life of Florence. However, when Lorenzo de' Medici's second son Giovanni was elected pope in 1513 under the name Pope Leo X, he restored the Medici family to power and made his younger brother Giuliano the new ruler of the city. From that point onwards, Florence was effectively controlled by the papacy until the sack of Rome at the hands of the Holy Roman Emperor Charles V (1500-1558) in 1527.

RIVALRY WITH MILAN AND ROME

The city of Milan was at that time the capital of a rich duchy founded by the Visconti dynasty, and had been governed by the Sforza family since 1450. Although it was not quite as influential as Florence, it was another major cultural hub, particularly from 1476 onwards, when it flourished under the leadership of Ludovico Sforza and entered a period of great political, economic, cultural and artistic prosperity. Although his court only counted a few high-ranking nobles, Sforza's aim was to become a worthy rival of Florence and the Medici family. However, he adopted a somewhat different strategy, and primarily focused on scientific research and entertainment rather than the arts, which only interested him insofar as they could be used to bolster his own position. However, his goal of turning Milan into a new Athens that all the greatest artists and philosophers of the era would flock to was jeopardised by threats to his grasp on power in the duchy. In 1500, during the Battle of Novara between Sforza and King Louis XII of France (1462-1515), Sforza's hired mercenaries – who had not been paid – handed him over to the French army, who imprisoned him in the Château de Loches. He died there in 1508.

Meanwhile, Rome and Florence were bitter rivals throughout the 15th century, as Rome was determined to extend its influence into Tuscany at any cost; however, all its efforts were in vain. The situation only changed when Giovanni de' Medici was elected pope, at which point Rome was finally able to exert control over Florence. As a result, it superseded Florence as the central hub of artistic influence in Italy at the start of the 16th century. Artistic patronage began to flourish in Rome, and a wealth of new buildings were constructed; St. Peter's Basilica was even demolished in 1505 so that it could be rebuilt, a process which lasted more than a century. The pope also summoned the greatest painters, sculptors and architects of the era (such as Bramante, Michelangelo and Raphael) to Rome to further enrich the city's artistic landscape, thus consolidating the city's political position and bolstering its reputation.

THE ITALIAN WARS

The end of the 15th century was marked by the Italian Wars (1494-1559), during which the Italian peninsula was invaded by the French.

In 1480, René of Anjou (King of Naples, 1409-1480) died without an heir and bequeathed his property to the French Crown. In 1492, King Charles VIII decided to claim this land and began the first Italian War (1494-1495), during which he captured the Kingdom of Naples. However, his enemies formed a coalition against him, meaning that he soon lost control of the territory and was forced to flee back to France.

His successor Louis XII (1462-1515) followed in his footsteps by claiming that, as the grandson of Valentina Visconti (1371-1408), he was the rightful heir to the Duchy of Milan. He conquered the city in 1499, taking Ludovico Sforza prisoner, and also captured the Kingdom of Naples with help from the Kingdom of Aragon. However, it once again proved impossible for France to maintain control over these territories due to newly-forged alliances between the country's enemies, and the Aragonese King Ferdinand II (1452-1516) gained control over Naples in 1504. However, the French finally consolidated their hold on Milan in 1515 with Francis I's victory in the Battle of Marignano.

The Italian Wars had significant cultural ramifications, as they brought French culture into close proximity with the art produced during the

Italian Renaissance. Certain Italian artists, including da Vinci, the architect Sebastiano Serlio (1475-1554), the sculptor Girolamo della Robbia (1488-1566), the artist Benvenuto Cellini (1500-1571) and the painter Francesco Primaticcio (1504-1570), spent time in France, Flanders and Germany, allowing Renaissance art to spread through the rest of Europe. Similarly, French artists such as the writer François Rabelais (1494-1553) and the poet Joachim Du Bellay (1522-1560) travelled to Italy to experience the culture of the Renaissance first-hand.

BIOGRAPHY

APPRENTICESHIP IN FLORENCE

Leonardo da Vinci was born in the village of Vinci in Tuscany on 15 April 1452. He was the illegitimate son of a notary named Piero da Vinci and a woman named Caterina, who was probably a servant. His mother raised him for the first four years of his life, after which he was sent to live with his father, who provided him with a simple education that consisted of reading, writing, arithmetic and basic Latin. During his youth he spent a great deal of time admiring the beauty of nature, and his grandmother instilled in him an appreciation for art, which he was able to see in Vinci and in the neighbouring towns.

Da Vinci had a gift for drawing and painting, and in 1469 he was taken on as one of the apprentices at the workshop of Andrea del Verrocchio (Italian artist, 1435-1488) in Florence, where he worked alongside artists like Sandro Botticelli and Domenico Ghirlandaio. His mentor began by teaching him basic painting techniques such as crushing pigments and creating resin. As time went on, da Vinci was permitted to assist Verrocchio with some of his own paintings: for example, he painted the angel on the left and the background of Verrocchio's painting *The Baptism of Christ* (1472-1475). During his time there, da Vinci also learned sculpture and goldsmithery.

Although he began to garner recognition for his work as a painter from 1472, the young artist continued to work closely with his master. He received his first public commission in 1478: an altarpiece for the Chapel of the Signoria in the Palazzo Vecchio of Florence, which was never completed. During the early stages of his career, da Vinci's work primarily consisted of sketches and paintings of the Virgin Mary and the nativity, and he was already starting to draw plans for a variety of mechanical devices.

A DISTINCTIVE MOTIF

Da Vinci's surname simply means "of Vinci", but the town itself was named after the osier willows that grew on the banks of the river that runs through it. These plants became something of a fascination for the artist, and their intertwined boughs both feature in his family crest and became a recurring motif in his paintings and sketches, most notably in the embroidered brocade on the *Mona Lisa*'s dress.

TRAVELLING TO MILAN

In spite of the high quality of his work, da Vinci did not catch the attention of the Medici family immediately. However, Lorenzo de' Medici sent him to Milan in 1482 to act as a cultural ambassador to Ludovico Sforza, and da Vinci remained in the city until 1499. This was the most active period of his career, during which he produced much of the work that made his name. For the most part, he worked on solving military and civil engineering issues and scientific research, although he also helped to organise a number of extravagant parties. This was also when he painted *The Last Supper* in the refectory of the convent of Santa Maria delle Grazie (between 1494 and 1498, to be precise), and he spent 16 years working on a monument in honour of the former Duke of Milan, Francesco Sforza (1401-1466), although it was never completed. Finally, he also opened his own workshop and took on a number of apprentices, including Giovanni Ambrogio de Predis (c. 1455-1508), Francesco Napoletano (c. 1470-1501) and Gian Giacomo Caprotti (c. 1480-1524), who was also known by his nickname Salai and was so devoted to da Vinci that he followed him to France.

In 1499, when Louis XII invaded the Duchy of Milan and took Ludovico Sforza captive, da Vinci left the city and returned to Florence. Along the way, he stopped in Mantua and spent some time at the court of the renowned patron of the arts Isabella d'Este (1474-1539), who tried in vain to convince him to remain there, then made another stop in Venice, where the authorities sought his advice on the city's new fortifications against the threat of an Ottoman invasion.

RETURN TO FLORENCE

Upon his return to Florence, da Vinci threw himself into a number of artistic, mechanical and scientific research projects, and received commissions from a range of patrons including the rulers of France, Venice and the Ottoman Empire. He made a number of brief trips to Rome, where he was consulted on where Michelangelo's *David* (1501-1504) should be placed and on the structural soundness of a number of important buildings. He later spent some time in Ferrara between 1502 and 1503, where he worked as a military engineer for Cesare Borgia, and travelled around the entire region of Romagna to study how the towns and fortresses there had been conquered in the past. During that time, he produced a number of highly accurate maps of Imola (a town located in the modern-day region of Emilia-Romagna in Italy) and of northern Italy as a whole. He eventually returned to Florence when Borgia's defeat at the hands of his enemy Pope Julius II (1443-1513) was imminent.

In 1503, da Vinci opened a new workshop in Florence, and was commissioned to paint a fresco in the grand council chamber of the Palazzo Vecchio depicting the Battle of Anghiari. Michelangelo was also commissioned to paint a second fresco in the same hall, which sparked a certain rivalry between the two artists. However, da Vinci's fresco has been lost; according to legend, it was hidden behind a false wall, although it may simply have been painted over, and it was left incomplete after an incident involving wax-based paints caused some of the colours to run and damaged the painting. Following this, da Vinci took a number of trips, visiting Piombino and Vinci in 1504 and Milan on a number of occasions in the following years. This was also when he began painting the famous *Mona Lisa*.

In 1507, da Vinci took on a new apprentice called Francesco Melzi (c. 1491-1570), whom he treated like a surrogate son. Melzi also proved utterly devoted to his mentor, even after his death.

RETIREMENT IN FRANCE

In 1508, da Vinci returned to Milan after being summoned there by Charles d'Amboise (French nobleman, 1473-1511), who was acting as governor of the duchy at that time at the behest of King Louis XII. This resulted in da Vinci being made "painter and engineer to the King of France", an official position which came with a hefty salary. However, this was also the period of his life when he produced the least artwork.

When Massimiliano Sforza (Italian duke, 1493-1530) reconquered Milan and ousted the French occupiers in 1512, da Vinci returned to Rome, as he was considered a French sympathiser and was therefore unwelcome. During his time in Rome, he chiefly focused on engineering projects, and worked alongside the likes of the artists Bramante, Michelangelo and Raphael.

In 1516, da Vinci left Rome and moved to Amboise in France on the invitation of King Francis I, bringing with him his notebooks and a handful of paintings, including the *Mona Lisa* and *The Virgin and Child with St. Anne*. The French king was a great admirer of da Vinci's genius, and granted him a generous stipend that enabled him to retire comfortably, as well as allowing him to stay in the Château de Clos Lucé in exchange for his company. Da Vinci continued to help coordinate both social gatherings and a variety of construction projects, including the Château de Chambord.

However, da Vinci's health was steadily deteriorating, and he was left unable to move his right arm towards the end of his life. He died in Clos Lucé on 2 May 1519, bequeathing his sketches and notes to his friend and pupil Francesco Melzi, his money to his siblings and his vineyard to Salai.

In his book *Leonardo da Vinci: A Memory of His Childhood* (1910), Sigmund Freud (Austrian psychoanalyst, 1856-1939) uses an anecdote from da Vinci's childhood as the basis for an analysis of the inventor's entire personality. According to Freud, da Vinci's paintings conceal telling signs of inner psychological complexes, especially his nostalgia for a close relationship with a mother figure, which Freud believed to be the reason for da Vinci's homosexuality. Of course, historians continue to debate the question of da Vinci's sexual orientation, although two court documents dating from 1476 contain details of a trial for sodomy, which was illegal at the time, in which da Vinci is named as one of the defendants and his relationship which Verrocchio is called into question. However, this case was dismissed on a legal technicality, and it has been speculated that the Medici family may have had some influence in ensuring its dismissal as well, given that one of the other defendants was associated with the family. Furthermore, many have speculated that the relationship between da Vinci and Salai was sexual in nature.

CHARACTERISTICS OF DA VINCI'S WORK

VERROCCHIO'S INFLUENCE

The years that da Vinci spent as Verrocchio's apprentice clearly influenced his painting style a great deal, as many of Verrocchio's signature techniques can also be seen in his protégé's work. In fact, even the most distinctive characteristic of da Vinci's work – namely the mysterious smile that appears in many of his portraits, most famously including the *Mona Lisa* – is actually also present in many of Verrocchio's works. However, while Verrocchio did not place any particular importance on this smile, da Vinci considered it a kind of reflection of the subject's soul (Santi, 1976: 62).

Furthermore, da Vinci's tendency to paint angelic faces crowned with a halo of gleaming hair can also be interpreted as a sign of Verrocchio's influence, and some of da Vinci's paintings seem to be directly inspired by his mentor's work. For example, his portrait *Ginevra de' Benci* (1475) is very similar to *Woman with Flowers* (1475-1480), a bust sculpted by Verrocchio.

Finally, da Vinci's preoccupation with using perspective to give his paintings depth and with accurately depicting volume by contrasting light and dark tones is probably also thanks to Verrocchio's influence. Verrocchio's reputation was primarily built on his talent as a sculptor, and he also schooled da Vinci in the techniques and particularities of that medium, which inspired his desire to make his paintings seem so three-dimensional that the viewer could almost believe that they could get a different view of them by walking around them. This characteristic is particularly striking in da Vinci's portraits.

PAINTING AS A SCIENCE

Although he drew a great deal of inspiration from his mentor, da Vinci's artistic process always featured somewhat unique and unprecedented elements.

His goal in each of his paintings was always to depict reality as accurately as possible by using a technique that was practically scientific in its precision and rigour. Before painting anything, he would spend hours or even days observing the people, animals or elements of the natural environment that he was intending to use as his subject and draw numerous sketches of them in order to analyse them in minute detail, filling countless notebooks with this important preparatory work. He always adopted the same approach: observe, repeat the observation from different angles and then draw what he saw. He also studied a number of sciences, including anatomy, botany, optics and geometry, and threw himself into practical work, which sometimes involved dissecting human and animal corpses in order to gain a better understanding of anatomical functions. He would then use his observations, notes, sketches and research to create incredibly lifelike works. He combined so many realistic details in his landscape paintings that they resulted in idyllic reproductions of nature that seemed to stretch on endlessly, a characteristic which was further accentuated by his use of the *sfumato* technique.

The extensive research that da Vinci regularly carried out led to artistic professions such as that of the painter being redefined to include a scientific dimension: henceforth, painting came to be seen as a science in its own right, or even as a supreme science which combined all others. The goal of painting was no longer to simply create a simple, static portrait of an individual, but to create a representation of their life as a whole and, above all, to depict reality as faithfully as possible. One particularly good example of this trend is da Vinci's *The Last Supper*, which depicts the emotions of the apostles in response to Jesus' announcement that one of them will betray him with striking realism. Movement and dynamism became essential aspects of art, particularly as a way of conveying the subjects' emotions. As such, the artist's anatomical observations were a valuable source of information, as his understanding of the human body enabled him to depict movement in an extremely realistic manner.

LEON BATTISTA ALBERTI

Leon Battista Alberti (1404-1472) was the foremost theoretician of the arts during the Italian Renaissance. He wrote a number of treatises on painting and architecture in which he laid out the principles of perspective and the importance of proportion, and he believed that all modern artists ought to be familiar with perspective, geometry and anatomy. As such, the idea of an innate link between art and a scientific method was already present in his work, which preceded that of da Vinci by several decades. Like many other artists of his time, da Vinci drew heavily on the principles laid out by Alberti.

MAJOR TECHNICAL INNOVATIONS

In addition to the fact that he was one of the first Italian artists to use oil paints, da Vinci also incorporated a number of innovative painting techniques into his work:

- He is most notably credited with developing the *sfumato* technique, which involves combining multiple microlayers of paint in order to create a smoky effect which mimics the contours of the body, making its shape seem more natural. It also makes it possible to create more nuances between different shades of colour in a very small section of the painting.

- The second major technical innovation attributed to da Vinci is atmospheric perspective, which involves using increasingly faded, blurred colours to create an illusion of distance and depth. This allows the foreground of the painting to be distinguished from the background without producing a jarring contrast between them and creates an impression of distant objects that almost seem to sink into the mists of the landscape.

Da Vinci also stands apart from earlier artists because of his conception of portraits and landscapes. He produced the first real landscape painting in the history of art, which was an ink sketch of the Arno Valley drawn in 1473. With just a few strokes of his pen and some simple shading, he managed to convey the rushing of the water along the riverbed and the wind blowing through the trees, cleverly using perspective and *chiaroscuro* (the interplay between light and shadow) to create a startlingly realistic image. Previously, landscapes were rarely painted at all, and only as a background for portraits, but in da Vinci's work it became the main subject of the painting.

Da Vinci's work on portraiture was also highly innovative. Although the genre itself was already very fashionable, da Vinci's approach was unprecedented: he introduced the concept of allegorical portraits, which used objects and colours to metaphorically represent the subject's inner world and used visual effects that hinted at movement. These effects included depicting the painting's subject against a dark backdrop, allowing the artist to play with light and making the subject stand out more, and by using the so-called "golden ratio", which involves arranging the elements of the painting to create a kind of spiral effect that draws the eye inward.

Finally, da Vinci was the first artist to use pyramidal composition, a technique which many later artists adopted. He was also extremely skilled at grouping the subjects of a painting together in an eye-catching manner and using the way these subjects look at each other to accentuate the connections between them and hint at the nature of the relationships between them.

NOTABLE WORKS

THE LAST SUPPER

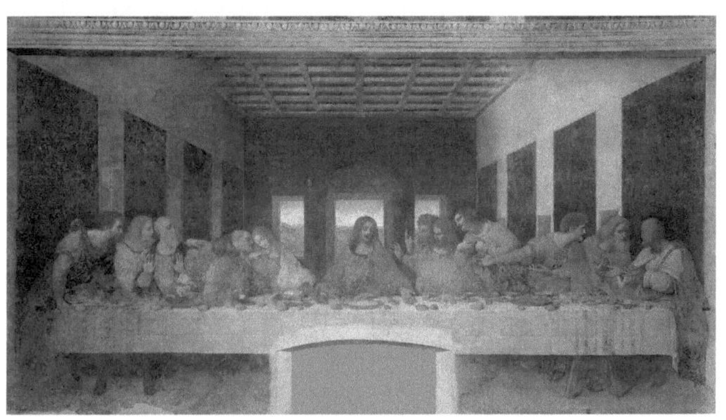

| *The Last Supper*, 1494-1498, fresco, 460 x 880 cm, Milan, refectory of the convent of Santa Maria delle Grazie.

The Last Supper was commissioned by Ludovico Sforza for the Dominican convent of Santa Maria delle Grazie in Milan. It depicts the moment during the first communion when Jesus revealed to his disciples that one of them would betray him, and uses an original composition. Creating a painting of 13 people clustered around a table is no easy task, and earlier artists had often depicted Judas on the opposite side of the table from the other apostles in order to set him apart from them. However, da Vinci broke with this tradition by seating Judas among the rest of the apostles at Jesus' right hand – the only thing that sets him apart from the others is his lack of reaction in response to Jesus' announcement.

The aspect of this enormous fresco that da Vinci chose to emphasise most is emotion. While previous artists who had depicted this scene had always focused on the event itself, da Vinci took an alternative approach by creating a veritable psychological analysis of each of the individuals in the painting through their gestures and facial expressions: one of the disciples is so stupefied that he has paused with his cup halfway to his lips, another radiates worry and concern, a third is so shocked he has knocked a glass over, and so on. The sheer variety of poses and expressions featured in the painting make it more than a work of art: it is also a study of human nature.

The Last Supper is also a masterclass in perspective: da Vinci does not simply follow the basic rules, but goes beyond them to create an even more realistic perspective which more closely imitates the way a human being sees the world. By making it seem as though the refectory itself melds into the scene depicted in the painting, the fresco creates the impression that the room is larger than it really is, and the inclusion of objects in the painting that mirrored the objects the nuns used in real life gives this illusion greater verisimilitude.

Unfortunately, *The Last Supper* has been very poorly preserved, partially because of the experimental technique used by da Vinci. Instead of using the traditional technique for painting a fresco, he used a mixture of oil and watercolour so that he would be able to touch up or modify the painting as desired. However, this meant that the painting quickly degraded, due in large part to the humidity in the room. Many attempts have been made to restore the original painting in the intervening centuries, but in most cases they have simply worsened the situation. Fortunately, the most recent restoration attempts in the 20th century have made use of new techniques that have allowed remnants of da Vinci's original painting to be restored.

A HIGHLY COVETED WORK

The Last Supper immediately garnered rapturous praise upon its completion: Francis I was so taken with it when he visited the convent that he went so far as to request that the wall be torn down so that the fresco could be moved to France, and the same demand was made by Napoleon I (French emperor, 1769-1821) many years later. However, in spite of these rulers' demands and the fact that the convent was practically destroyed when it was bombed in 1943, *The Last Supper* remains in its original location today.

THE *MONA LISA*

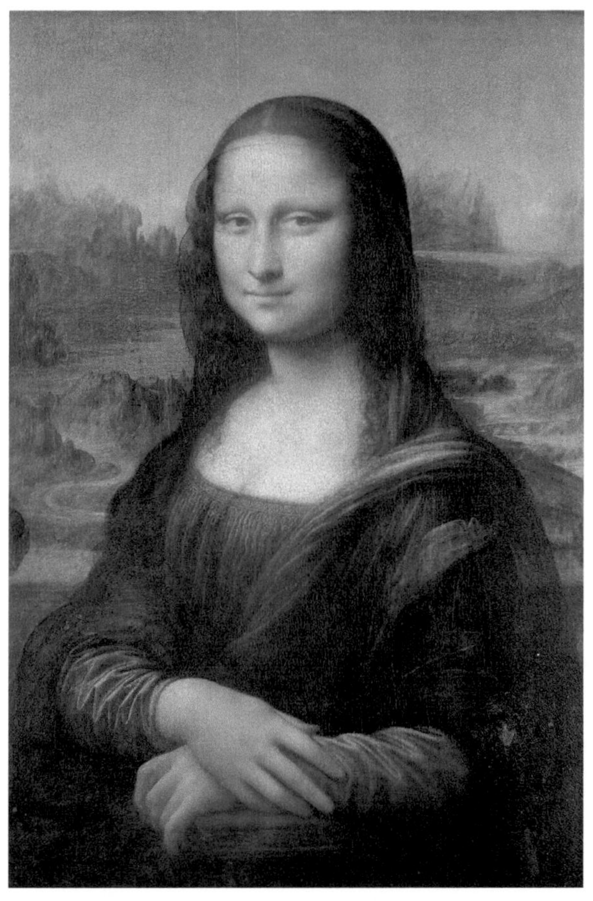

| *Mona Lisa*, 1503-1505, oil painting on wooden panel, 77 x 53 cm, Paris, Louvre Museum.

This painting is assumed to depict Lisa del Giocondo (Italian noblewoman, 1479-1542), the wife of a Florentine silk merchant named Francesco del Giocondo who is believed to have commissioned the painting from da Vinci. However, it seems that he never received the finished work, as da Vinci bequeathed the painting to his pupil Salai, who sold it to Francis I in 1518. Modern radiography has indicated that the painting was retouched on multiple occasions, showing that da Vinci was constantly in search of perfection.

This is the earliest known portrait by an Italian artist which depicts a subject within such a large frame: the subject's entire torso is visible, and there is even a gap between her and the sides of the painting. The young woman is depicted leaning forward slightly, which makes it seem as though the viewer can see her from multiple angles, and she gazes directly at the viewer, her eyes and smile seeming to gleam with both irony and wisdom. Her position in the foreground of the painting makes her seem larger than life, which is almost disconcerting in such a small painting. However, this accentuates her charm and calm demeanour, although she also exudes a certain degree of aloofness.

The landscape in the background is imaginary. It is interesting to note that the two lines of the horizon on each side of the subject's head are not quite in line with each other, which draws the viewer's attention to the subject's smile and makes it appear as though she is concealing a laugh. Her smile is the focal point of the entire painting, and it almost seems as though the rest of the portrait was only painted to complement and frame it. This smile could reflect so many different thoughts that it gives the woman a timeless, almost universal quality. It also adds to the mystery that still surrounds the portrait: why was Mona Lisa smiling, and why did da Vinci paint this portrait? These questions remain unanswered to this day, despite the myriad theories about the young woman's identity that have sprung up over the years. Thanks to her preternatural beauty, she has been called everything from the perfect woman to a vampire, a sphinx, a siren, a Madonna, a prostitute or a hermaphrodite, but one thing is certain: the combination of her enigmatic smile and the dreamlike landscape behind her transform this work of art from a mere portrait to something approaching perfection.

Finally, da Vinci's use of *sfumato* is particularly masterful in this painting, and allows him to create a perfect harmony between Mona Lisa and the landscape behind her. For example, the aqueduct in the distance on the right-hand side of the painting seems like an extension of the scarf thrown over her shoulder, and the curls of her hair almost blur into the rocks on the left-hand side.

L.H.O.O.Q.

The *Mona Lisa* is probably the most famous painting in the world, which is due in no small part to the attention it received when it was stolen from the Louvre in 1911 by Vincenzo Peruggia (1881-1925), an Italian worker who wanted to bring the portrait back to his homeland. Furthermore, the painting provided a starting-point for many artists who wanted to challenge the conventions of traditional art and gave rise to numerous parodies, the most famous of which is probably the painting *L.H.O.O.Q.* (1919) by

Marcel Duchamp (French-American artist, 1887-1968), which is a near-exact replica of da Vinci's work, save for the beard and moustache scribbled over the Mona Lisa's face.

VIRGIN OF THE ROCKS

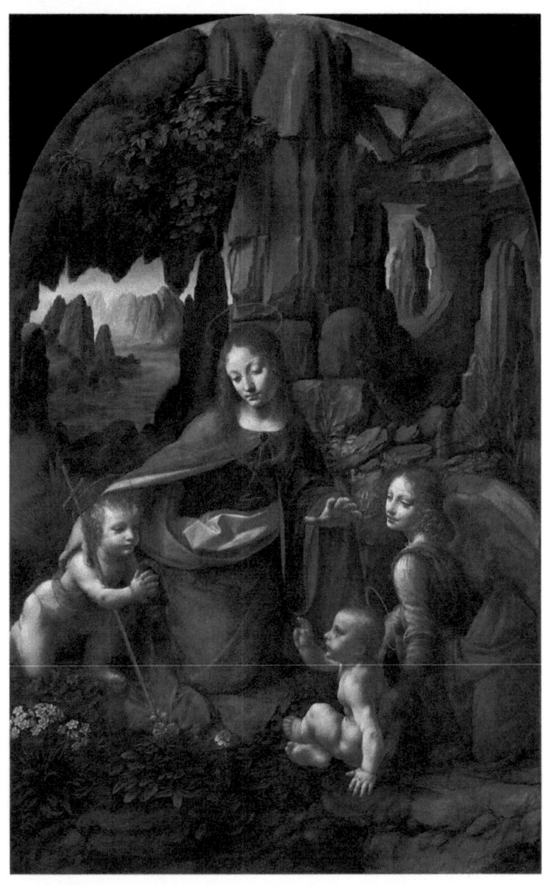

| *Virgin of the Rocks*, 1495-1508, oil painting on wooden panel, 189.5 x 120 cm, London, National Gallery.

There are two versions of this painting: the earlier version, which dates from 1488, is kept at the Louvre in Paris, while the later version is exhibited at the National Gallery in London. The latter forms the central panel of a triptych altarpiece which was designed for the Chapel of the Immaculate Conception in the church of San Francesco Maggiore in Milan. The side panels are decorated with two angels painted by da Vinci's students.

The later version of the painting is more detailed and features more innovative styles. In fact, it reflects many of the conventions that would come to define 16th-century art, as it features imposing figures and the interplay between light and shadow creates contrasts which emphasise the subjects' physiques. It is also one of the earliest examples of a pyramidal composition: the Virgin Mary forms the top of the pyramid, while the angel and the two children (Christ on the right and John the Baptist on the left) seated below her form its sides and base. Furthermore, each individual seems less passive than in the first version, and their facial expressions reflect their emotions: the Virgin Mary's gentle features convey maternal affection, while Jesus' earnestness is made clear by the confidence and intensity with which he gives his blessing. Finally, the setting seems much more mystical, which confers greater importance on the scene taking place.

The rocky landscape takes on a metaphorical significance in this painting: the cavern entrance represents both the mother's womb and the Allegory of the Cave as set out by Plato (Greek philosopher, c. 424-348 BCE). This backdrop acts as a protected, isolated location where the characters can come together as a whole. As such, the painting does not depict a specific Biblical event, nor does it exclusively refer to the Immaculate Conception; on the contrary, it can be interpreted in many different ways, from a representation of the creation of the world to the discovery and propagation of knowledge. Furthermore, the left corner of the background seems to offer the viewer a glimpse of open, infinite space. However, every aspect of the painting has been made to look extremely realistic.

This is arguably da Vinci's most enigmatic painting, as it raises a number of unanswered questions: what is the symbolic meaning of the painting? How should the poses of its subjects be interpreted? Could it be said to feature elemental symbolism (earth, water, air and fire)? Does it represent the sum of all knowledge? The list of questions goes on and on, but da Vinci left no clues that hint at his original intentions, so the potential interpretations of the painting are limited only by our imaginations.

THE VIRGIN AND CHILD WITH ST. ANNE

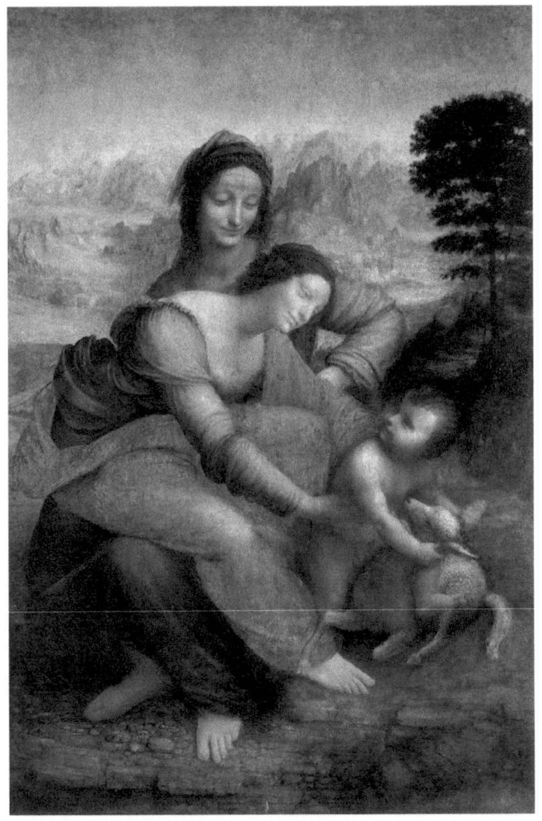

| *The Virgin and Child with St. Anne*, c. 1510, oil painting on wooden panel, 168 x 130 cm, Paris, Louvre Museum.

The idea for this painting took a firm grip on da Vinci's mind as early as 1500, when he began sketching numerous variations of a picture featuring the Virgin Mary, Jesus and St. Anne. The scene that it depicts is imaginary, not Biblical, as St. Anne (who was Mary's mother, according to apocryphal tradition) died before Jesus was born. As such, the painting takes on a symbolic meaning, wherein St. Anne's presence represents the completion of a trinity spanning three generations. The painting was commissioned as an altarpiece for the Church of Santissima Annunziata in Florence, presumably by King Louis XII when his daughter Claude was born in 1499, given that his wife's name was Anne. However, the painting remained unfinished and was never delivered.

The painting's composition is extremely dynamic: its subjects are in motion rather than fixed in place, and the water really seems to be flowing over the mountains in the background. It is also a clear example of pyramidal composition, with St. Anne and the Virgin Mary seeming to form one solid shape. Mary is dressed in vivid shades of red and blue, and sits on her mother's lap with her arms outstretched towards her son, thus acting as a connection between all three generations, and this bond is reinforced by the diagonal line that can be traced through their gazes. Furthermore, Mary's right arm seems to extend from the same position as St. Anne's, and the line of her left arm continues into Jesus'. By positioning the painting's subjects in this way, the manner in which Mary is reaching for her son appears almost distorted.

Furthermore, St. Anne's arm is positioned in a way that makes it seem as though she is cradling a child, and Mary's head appears to be resting on her mother's shoulder as though she were a young child. Meanwhile, the lamb represents the Passion, meaning the sacrifice that Jesus will make later in life. The smiles on the women's faces convey maternal affection, which attests to the bond between all three individuals and to their desire to protect each other. The fact that they are all looking at each other emphasises the unity of the group, but also creates a sense of isolation: this scene almost seems removed from the mortal world, and a chasm separates the painting's subjects from the viewer. This impression is reinforced by the mountains stretching skyward in the background, which makes the landscape seem endless. Da Vinci's use of *sfumato* creates a series of glazes that combine to form an unusual shade of blue, and atmospheric perspective makes St. Anne – and, by extension, the rest of the group – seem to fade into the background and become one with it, particularly on the right-hand side of the painting, where the hues of colour are more subtle and the objects depicted are further apart.

Finally, da Vinci uses *chiaroscuro* to create fabric that seems both light but rich in colour, and which hugs the forms of the bodies below it; for example, the shape of Mary's right leg can be seen through her dress. Da Vinci also uses this technique to highlight their smiles and benevolent expressions.

DA VINCI'S LEGACY

The influence da Vinci has had on other artists, even during his own lifetime, cannot be overstated. His frequent travels gave him the opportunity to meet many other important figures of the era, and he left a strong impression on each of them. Furthermore, his interests were so varied that his research, discoveries and inventions had a tremendous impact on many different fields.

The students he taught were the first individuals to help spread his influence. Before long, these painters made a name for themselves as the "Leonardeschi", because in spite of the fact that they were scattered all over the Mediterranean region, their works all retained a degree of similarity to their mentor's, particularly through the use of *sfumato* and enigmatic smiles. The best-known artists in this group were Giovanni de Predis (1455-1508), Giovanni Boltraffio (1467-1516) and Cesare da Sesto (1477-1523).

Da Vinci also influenced Raphael a great deal. For example, the latter's *Portrait of Maddalena Doni*

(1506) bears many similarities to da Vinci's *Mona Lisa*: the subject's posture is identical, the composition is similar and the way the background fades to blue is very reminiscent of da Vinci's work. Raphael also imitated da Vinci's pyramidal composition, notably in *Madonna and Child with Saint John the Baptist* (1505-1508), and adopted techniques such as *sfumato* and *chiaroscuro*, for example in the *Madonna del Granduca* (1504-1505). Like da Vinci, he grouped the subjects of the painting together, used visual cues to express their relationships with each other and idealised nature by depicting it as an infinite space.

The work of the German painter Albrecht Dürer (1471-1528) also attests to the influence of the Italian polymath to such an extent that he was nicknamed "the Leonardo of the North". Dürer was primarily interested in da Vinci's research on the subjects of anatomy, proportions and natural science, as well in his blueprints for military inventions and his signature interlacing patterns.

Da Vinci's contributions to science are equally numerous, and even his sketches based on observation revolutionised several different scientific fields. Thanks to the precision and accuracy of his botanical sketches, da Vinci is sometimes considered the father of modern botany, and he was the first individual to identify how sedimentary rocks and marine fossils are formed. His dissections led to several discoveries in the field of anatomy, particularly with regard to the heart, and aided with the development of techniques which allowed for greater progress to be made in that field in subsequent years. In addition, his research and inventions were used as the basis for many later inventions, including some major innovations such as the steam engine.

After his death, da Vinci came to be seen as an almost godlike figure, due in no small part to the biography that was written about him by Giorgio Vasari (Italian artist and writer, 1511-1574) in *Lives of the Most Excellent Painters, Sculptors and Architects* (1550-1568). However, in the following centuries, many artists rebelled against the conventions of traditional art, of which da Vinci was generally seen as the figurehead. As such, da Vinci's work was generally held in contempt from the time of John Ruskin (English art critic, 1819-1900) onwards, and Auguste Renoir (French artist, 1841-1919) openly stated that da Vinci's work bored him. When Freud published his psychoanalysis of da Vinci in 1910, it came as a relief to the art world to know that even the quintessential Renaissance man was not perfect, merely a mortal who could be equalled or even surpassed.

Not all modern artists feel the need to distance themselves from da Vinci's work: the members of the Futurist movement that emerged in Italy in the early 20th century adopted similar theories to da Vinci's, even though they were vocal critics of the *Mona Lisa*. In any case, da Vinci continues to inspire passionate debate even now, five centuries after his death, and remains the object of great fascination. To this day, his legacy acts as an endless font of inspiration for new artistic theories and thought.

SUMMARY

- Leonardo da Vinci was born in Tuscany in 1452. Although his parents were not married, his father acknowledged him as his son and raised him in his own household, and he was granted an apprenticeship in the workshop of Andrea del Verrocchio in Florence in 1469 thanks to his talent for painting and drawing.
- In 1482, he travelled to Milan as an ambassador to Ludovico Sforza, who was the ruler of the city at that time. He remained in the city for the following 17 years, which constituted the most productive period of his life, and it was during this time that he painted *The Last Supper*, a fresco that adorns the wall of the refectory in the convent of Santa Maria delle Grazie.
- After this, he returned to Florence and entered the service of Cesare Borgia, then travelled back to Milan before spending some time in the Vatican. He then left Italy for good and settled in Amboise in France, which was also the home of the French monarch, Francis I. Da Vinci died there in 1519.

- Da Vinci's interests were extremely varied. He was fascinated by everything from anatomy to geology, optics, botany, architecture, painting, sculpture and engineering. As such, he is generally considered the quintessential "Renaissance man", meaning a highly accomplished polymath.

- He developed a unique artistic process which reflected his boundless curiosity: he would spend long periods of time observing the world around him and making notes about his observations, sketching and developing theories which he wrote out in a series of notebooks, filling thousands of pages. This approach, based on extensive research and meticulous observation, allowed him to transform art into a veritable science.

- His artistic style was heavily influenced by his mentor, Verrocchio, from whom he borrowed a number of techniques and motifs, including the distinctive smile that his work is famous for. However, he also developed new techniques, including pyramidal composition, *sfumato* (which creates a smoky effect around the subject's body) and atmospheric perspective (which involves gradually blurring shapes and colours together in order to set the foreground of a painting apart from the background). He was also one of the first artists to depict landscapes as a subject in their own right, and pioneered the practice of using allegory in portraits.

We want to hear from you!
Leave a comment on your online library
and share your favourite books on social media!

FURTHER READING

BIBLIOGRAPHY

- Alberti de Mazzeri, S. (1984) *Léonard de Vinci. L'homme et son temps*. Paris: Payot.

- Arasse, D. (2005) *Leonardo da Vinci*. Saybrook: Konecky & Konecky.

- Bramly, S. (1991) *Discovering the Life of Leonardo da Vinci*. New York: HarperCollins.

- Brioist, P. (2011) *Léonard de Vinci. Arts, sciences et techniques*. Paris: La Documentation française.

- Debolini, F. (2000) *Léonard de Vinci*. Paris: La Martinière.

- Fride-Carrassat, P. (2004) *Great Painters*. Edinburgh: Chambers Arts Library.

- Koering, J. (2007) *Léonard de Vinci. Dessins et peintures*. Paris: Hazan.

- (2008) Léonard De Vinci : un sacré bonhomme. *Historia Thématique*. 113.

- MacCurdy, E. (1906) *Leonardo da Vinci's Notebooks*. London: Duckworth & Co.

- Marani, P. (2003) *Leonardo da Vinci: The Complete Paintings*. New York: Harry N. Abrams.

- Murray, L. (1978) The High Renaissance and
  Mannerism: Italy, the North and Spain 1500-1600.
  London: Thames et Hudson.

- Santi, B. (1978) *Leonardo da Vinci*. Edinburgh:
  Constable.

- Vezzosi, A. (1997) *Leonardo da Vinci: Renaissance
  Man*. London: Thames and Hudson.

- Wallace, R. (1966) *The World of Leonardo: 1452-1519*.
  London: Little, Brown.

ADDITIONAL SOURCES

- *Leonardo*. (2003) [TV Mini Series]. Sarah Aspinall,
  Tim Dunn, Nicholas Rossiter. Dir. UK: BBC.

- *The Da Vinci Detective*. (2006) [Documentary].
  Nigel Levy. Dir. UK: Channel 4, Darlow Smithson,
  RTÉ.

- Leonardo. *Understanding Art: Hidden Lives of
  Works of Art*. (2011) [Documentary episode]. Stan
  Neumann. France: ARTE France.

- *Inside the Mind of Leonardo*. (2013) [Documentary].
  Julian Jones. Dir. UK: Handel Productions/IWC
  Media.

ICONOGRAPHIC SOURCES

- *The Last Supper*, 1494-1498, fresco, 460 x 880 cm, Milan, refectory of the convent of Santa Maria delle Grazie. Royalty-free reproduction picture.

- *Mona Lisa*, 1503-1505, oil painting on wooden panel, 77 x 53 cm, Paris, Louvre Museum. Royalty-free reproduction picture.

- *Virgin of the Rocks*, 1495-1508, oil painting on wooden panel, 189.5 x 120 cm, London, National Gallery. Royalty-free reproduction picture.

- *The Virgin and Child with St. Anne*, c. 1510, oil painting on wooden panel, 168 x 130 cm, Paris, Louvre Museum. Royalty-free reproduction picture.

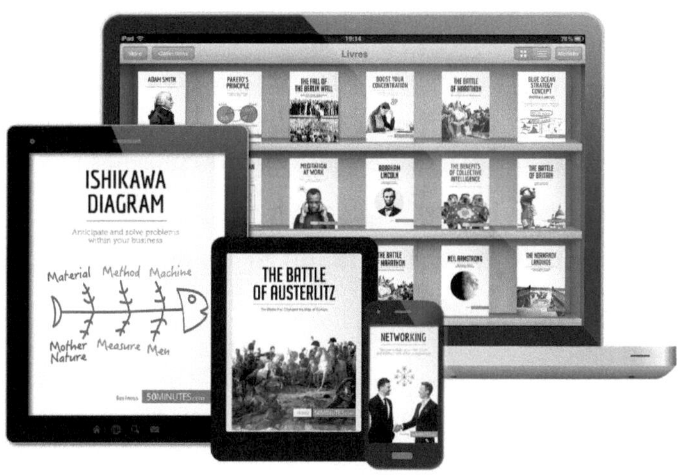
50MINUTES.com
History
Business
Coaching
Book Review
Health & Wellbeing
ISHIKAWA DIAGRAM
Anticipate and solve problems within your business
Material Method Machine
Mother Nature Measure Men
THE BATTLE OF AUSTERLITZ
NETWORKING
IMPROVE YOUR GENERAL KNOWLEDGE
IN A BLINK OF AN EYE !
www.50minutes.com

www.50minutes.com

Ebook EAN: 9782808011082

Paperback EAN: 9782808011099

Legal Deposit: D/2018/12603/296

Cover: © *Head of a Girl* (c. 1483) by Leonardo da Vinci; © *Head of a Woman* (c. 1500-1510) by Leonardo da Vinci.

Digital conception by Primento, the digital partner of publishers.